The Too-tight Tutu

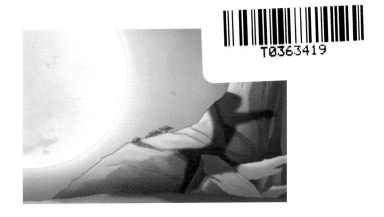

Written by Nancy O'Connor

Illustrated by Omar Aranda

Flying Start
to Literacy®

Contents

Chapter 1:
Lion's problem

Lion was king of the animals. It was almost time for his birthday party and all the animals were expecting a fantastic party.

But Lion had a big problem – he wasn't happy with this year's plans.

He had a band of zebras and a group
of acrobatic monkeys, but Lion wanted
something more.

One evening, Lion went for a walk to think.
Suddenly, he stopped. In the moonlight,
high on a hill, he could see the shadow
of a dancer. Lion watched the shadow
as it danced gracefully.

That was what his birthday party needed –
dancing!

"Excuse me," said Lion.

The shadow froze and then it disappeared.

"Come back!" roared Lion. "Please come back!"

He raced to the top of the hill, but all he
found was a pink tutu and a cloud of dust.

Chapter 2:
The too-tight tutu

The next morning, Lion called a meeting of all the animals.

"At this year's party, there will be dancing," said Lion.

All the animals were excited. The zebras brayed and the monkeys chattered.

"Hush," Lion ordered. "I am looking for the dancer I saw in the moonlight last night."

He held up the tutu for all to see.

"The dancer ran off but left behind this lovely tutu. I want her to dance at my party."

"I can dance," said Giraffe.

She slipped her head into the tutu,
but she could tug it only a short way
down her long neck.

Then she galloped, moving her head from
side to side.

In the trees, the monkeys began to laugh
and chatter:
"No, no, it's not true.
That tutu is too tight for you!"

"I am a graceful dancer," snorted Hippo,
still wet from the watering hole.
"You should see me dance in the water."

Hippo tried on the tutu, but only one of her
thick, grey legs would fit in it. And
then she stepped into the watering hole.

The monkeys waved their long arms
in the air and shrieked:
"Silly Hippo, that's not true.
That tutu is too tight for you!"

"Let me have the tutu," said Elephant.
"I am a lovely dancer."

Elephant slipped her trunk into the tutu.
She flapped her ears and swung her trunk.
Softly and silently, she swayed forwards and
backwards, and forwards and backwards.

The monkeys wagged their fingers
at Elephant and chanted:
"No, no, that won't do.
That tutu is too tight for you!"

Chapter 3:
Whose tutu?

"Stop!" roared Lion. "Enough!"

The animals were silent.

"This tutu is too tight for all of you. Whose tutu is it?" he demanded.

Finally, a big brown gnu cleared his throat.

"Ahem," he said. "I know who the tutu belongs to."

"Who? Who?" cried all the animals.

The gnu pointed to a shy little meerkat hiding in a burrow in the ground.

"You?" cried Giraffe. "You're too short."

"You?" cried Hippo. "You're too thin."

"You?" cried Elephant. "You're too small."

Lion pulled his long whiskers and stared at the little meerkat.

"Well . . . go ahead," he said finally. "Try it on."

"Try it on!   Try it on!" chanted the monkeys.

Chapter 4:
A perfect fit

The meerkat stepped out of her burrow
and slipped into the pink tutu.
It fit her perfectly.

All the animals gasped.
The monkeys clapped and cheered:
"The gnu knew! It's true, it's true.
That tutu was made just for you!"

The band of zebras began to play music. The meerkat stood up tall on her two hind legs. And then she danced in her pink tutu, leaping and turning.

When the music came to an end, she curtseyed before Lion. He took her tiny paw in his and smiled.

"Will you dance at my party?" he asked.

"It would be an honour, your Majesty," said the meerkat.

That year, the party was the grandest ever.

The band of zebras played the music
and all the animals sang along.
The monkeys performed acrobatics.

But when the meerkat danced in the moonlight, the animals whispered among themselves:

"It's true, it's true.

That tutu was made just for you!"